I0504652

THE SECRET ONLINE DOOR

BY

DAN PORTIK

Copyright ©2020 Dan Portik

TABLE OF CONTENTS

Introduction

After searching for ten years, I found a secret online door. It's a door that has opened up unbelievable opportunities that would never have been possible if I had given up my quest. This door has allowed me to reach almost anyone at any level and get everything I have requested of them. This door opens almost every time I try it because I've not only found the door, but I have located its key.

As I go through this door, I am in front of exactly who I want to meet, and, in most cases, the person or group I am speaking with is happy to meet me and willing to help me get whatever I ask for. This may sound like an affirmation of something to aspire to, but it's not. It's the truth of my experience.

Note that I'm not talking about a physical door here. It is a virtual door only used by those who are willing to do what it takes to find it, and use the key to step through it. To find and open the door for yourself requires a combination of research, tracking, and negotiating, paired with specifically timed online communication techniques. The techniques spark emotions and get people at any level to take notice *and* take action. That may make it sound a bit complicated, but if I can do it, so can you. I will break it down further on in the book. You will see exactly what to do, how to do it, and when to do it.

How have I done this? Primarily by trial and error. I learned valuable lessons from every wrong door or ineffective communication. Changes were made in my strategy. Variations in wording were tested, revised and tested again until I developed a strategy and process that works.

The results I've gotten from using the key to this door have worked for me both as a consumer and as a businessperson. The results have ranged from getting a very poor quality yard service company to have a regional manager fly in to personally reseed dead spots in my grass, to getting the senior vice president of one of the largest computer companies in the world take my unsatisfactory laptop back after I used it for over a year *and* give me a 50% discount *off wholesale* on a new purchase. I've gone through this door all the way up to contacting, presenting to, and co-authoring a book with a best-selling, world-renowned author and then becoming a best-selling author myself, without ever having written a book before.

Perhaps you're one of the many people who search the web to simply find information such as recipes, sports scores, or the day's news and, of course, a few YouTube videos. Perhaps you only go online to look up what's happening on your social media pages— keeping up with friends and family. That's all well and good, but there are so many more benefits you can gain online.

You can use the web to get what you want (and I don't just mean by shopping on Amazon). You can receive a higher level of service from businesses you use rather than accepting everything at face value. And, you can reach out to anyone at any level of celebrity or financial status, and get their attention.

I'm old enough to have experienced those hard rejections inherent in reaching out by phone and through in-person visits. Talk about saving time, saving face, and getting the job done…the doorway that has been created by the internet is the best thing that's happened to all of us! It is an avenue to achieve so much more than anyone could have imagined with conventional means of communication. On the other side of the secret online door is a road map straight to people we could never meet in person or call on the phone. The internet is such a powerful tool that I believe is under-valued and under-utilized by most. Online, you can communicate one-on-one with anyone and negotiate, in many cases, exactly what you want or need from them. Your results depend solely on your approach.

The point of this book is to show you that contacting and negotiating online with others is an art that can be mastered by anyone. I will teach you how to effectively communicate and get what you want, even when you can't hear voice inflection or see body language of the other people. Online communication has become the way of the world. It's simply more convenient to communicate online than in-person or by phone. To be successful in business and in life, we must communicate with others the way they want to be communicated with. It's time for us to become experts in online communication and negotiation.

Chapter 1

Building Your Path to the Secret Door

Before using the secret door, whether for business or personal matters, it's important to set the stage for what others will see online about you. You want to set up your own online profiles to enhance your own credibility before asking others for anything. Most of those you communicate with online will take at least a few minutes to look into who you are, and determine if you're for real or some crazy person who spends their time trying to get something for nothing. When you have a *professional* online presence, you will be taken more seriously by those you reach out to. I covered this in great detail in my book, "The Simple Path to Creating a Powerful, Professional Online Presence." I'll teach you enough here to get you started.

First impressions are everything online. Think of it this way, you wouldn't attend a ballet in jeans and a T-shirt, or interview for a job as vice president of a bank wearing a bathing suit. Well, you could attempt to get a job in a bathing suit, but your odds of landing that position would be slim to none. The same goes for reaching out to people online. Before you can ever communicate with anyone of authority online about anything, you must look as though you are someone that is of a caliber to be taken seriously.

Put yourself on the opposite side of an online conversation. If you are trying to reach someone to help you, how much time and effort do you think they'll put into your request if your profile picture on your social media platforms is of you chasing your dog around the yard with a can of beer in your hand? Now, if it's your job to host events for a beer company that's courting dog owners, it *might* be OK, but you would need to have something in your bio to explain it.

Remember, you can't make a first impression twice. One of the easiest ways to know if you are being seen properly is to have others look you up online and see what they can dig up on you. You might be shocked at what they find. Also, look at the people you are trying to reach. Look at their websites, or anything else online about them. I assure you if it's anyone of stature, their website and social channels will have a professional design. All their photos, videos and messaging will be carefully vetted and have the same look as well. There will be a continuity to everything as if it were planned. (And yes, it was planned in most cases, out to the very last detail.) Model what they're doing.

It's helpful to have your own domain name and personal website. When you do, it shows people you're serious about demonstrating professionalism. If you have an uncommon name, it's easy to get the domain name. Mine, for example, is danportik.com. This is not very common, so it was easy to get the domain and build a site. Also, always try to get the dot-com. This helps smooth your path through the secret door. There are many services out there to help you build a professional-looking site—even if it's only a single page. If you're not an expert in design, rely on those who are.

Connecting with Gatekeepers

Almost every high-profile individual has a personal assistant or someone who assists them with all of the functions of their lives and businesses. These are the gatekeepers. The gatekeepers themselves can be very well hidden, but can become quite accessible once you discover them. When attempting to reach people via phone or mail, you are at the mercy of many time-tested screening techniques to stop you from reaching your intended party. Before we talk about how to reach and get through gatekeepers online, you must first be aware that they are there. Your best bet is to never leave any stone unturned in finding ways to reach others.

The interesting thing about gatekeepers is that many of them know each other. Their high-profile bosses or leaders are connected on one level, and the gatekeepers (who often are the ones who get "stuff" done) are connected on another level. Once you reach one gatekeeper and prove yourself, the secret door may open to many more!

In my case of working with Tom Hopkins' organization, once I proved to his team that I was a reputable person who followed through with what I said I would do, introductions were made to other speakers and their gatekeepers. To me, trust is one of the most precious attributes to earn with anyone. Though it can be the hardest to earn, it's also the easiest to lose. Be willing to work hard for it and even harder to keep it.

Connecting with Influencers

In some cases, getting to the person you want to communicate with involves a roundabout strategy. There's nothing wrong with this. If you've tried the direct route and failed, look for someone else who is connected to that person and reach out to *them*. You might find that John Smith has a photo of Joe Celebrity on his Facebook page. If they're tennis partners or co-chairs of a charity event, they will know how to reach each other. If you can't go directly to Joe Celebrity, start by connecting with John Smith. Build trust with him, then ask for an introduction to Joe.

Consider connecting with several people at Joe Celebrity's company. Once you've built trust, you may be able to strike a chord with them that plays out in getting an introduction to the celebrity or someone who has that celebrity's ear.

Earning Trust

A certain degree of trust is required for any door to open. The person on the other side has to trust that you are who you say you are and that what you say is true. According to *The Stoic Emperor,* "Trust is slowly built. Trust is destroyed quickly. Trust can make complex things possible. Trust powers relationships, businesses and nations."

I have a friend who owns a music studio. Over the years, he has earned the trust of many rock stars whose names you would recognize. However, they all know they can trust him not to reveal their true identities, or information on projects they're working on. Being trustworthy has allowed him to hold the keys to many a secret online door and to grow his business.

Whether you're seeking to gain business or handle a customer service issue, you must prove yourself trustworthy. Never come across as someone wanting to take advantage of a situation. That's the fast track to getting the secret online doors I'll be teaching you about locked against your entry.

Be open, honest and forthright in all of your communications through the secret online doors and you will be able to get at the very least what you want, and possibly more than you ever dreamed of.

Chapter 2

The Advantages and Disadvantages of Communicating Online using the Secret Door

As with anything, there are both advantages and disadvantages to communicating and negotiating online.

Advantages

1. You can find out anything about anybody before you reach out to them through the secret door. It's as if you have a magic wand or a crystal ball, and you're the only one that knows it exists or knows how to use it.

2. One of the real advantages to online negotiating is that you don't always need to converse in real time. This is great for those of us who aren't great at thinking on our feet. We can pause, reflect, research, and find exactly the right words and techniques to use before sending or replying to messages. Plus, the web is an open book, if you know where to look.

3. Communicating online allows you to take some of the emotion out of a negotiation. Those on the other side of the negotiation won't be able to "read" your body language or hear your voice inflection. If they can't grasp your emotions, they are forced to make assumptions. This will likely be to your benefit. If, after receiving a quote for services you reply, "Wow, we didn't realize it was going to cost that much." They don't know

whether you are screaming it and punching holes in the walls or saying it while smiling about how low it is.

As a side note to this, you as the sender of online communication do have some say in how the receiver of your message will interpret your feelings. For example, if you send a message that reads, "Wow, we didn't realize it was going to cost that much," think of all the different ways that can be interpreted. Let's say you included an exclamation point at the end. That's a way to add emotion, but what emotion does it mean for you versus what it means for the recipient? How about if your reply was in all CAPITAL LETTERS? Most would interpret that as shouting. But are you shouting for joy? Or are you angry? This could be interpreted either way, couldn't it? Use this to your advantage!

4. You have the luxury of time on your side. Let's say you are conversing with a salesperson who gives you a price you don't like, and you reply, "Wow, we didn't realize it was going to cost that much." Your salesperson has a few options here. A pro is going to pick up the phone and call you to clarify what is going on. However, an average salesperson may email back and say, "Oh, I'm sorry for the misunderstanding. Is there a number or range you were thinking of that will move things forward?"

In reality, a truly good salesperson would have prequalified your budget long before it got to this point. But, let's say, for the time being, they did not. So, let's say the salesperson just emails back: "Oh, I didn't realize this was an issue. How about we take 10% off?" Just by being patient, you've gained an edge.

Believe it or not, open-ended replies will happen most of the time. There will be a broad, vague, counter-offer that leaves open all kinds of additional negotiating.

9

For example, a salesperson offering another 10% off is broad and open-ended. You now know this person has the authority to offer discounts, and believe me, they never offer their best amount first. You might respond with "10% is better, but my budget was really closer to 20% less. However, I would still need to run that by my wife." In essence, you're asking for more than 10% and you're creating another delay before the purchase will be made.

Every minute, hour, or day that you wait to answer allows the person on the other end of the conversation to think. About what? Well about what you are thinking. Or "what might I have done better to make this deal run smoother?" Or it might be something like. "Is that person still interested? Is he/she even still working at the company?" The longer you wait, the more your opponent will be thinking about the situation. So, keep that in mind the next time you are in negotiation with someone online. Time is on your side, not theirs.

One last side note: Don't wait *too long* to respond. If your amateur salesperson sends a second or third follow up email and doesn't hear back from you, they'll assume you don't want to continue the conversation, and move on to handling another client's needs. It's best not to leave them hanging. Keep them interested so you can get the best deal possible.

Disadvantages

1. You won't be able to take everything you find online about others at face value. If you've spent any time at all on Facebook, you'll know that most people only share their "wonderful" vacations, "incredible" family time, and such. Real life isn't all roses and sunshine. And, there are people who will create incredible profiles for themselves with less-than-truthful details. On LinkedIn, in particular, people have

been known to exaggerate their academic lives and honors received.

2. The time lag in communication could be a disadvantage. When all parties are in the same room, or on a conference call together, negotiations can go back and forth rather quickly. Communicating online allows each party to take their time about replying—maybe even allowing them to consult with someone else who is better at negotiating. This can create stress on either side of the negotiation. And when you're negotiating, keeping a low stress level is important to try to keep the communication flowing.

3. Not having those visual cues, most people will go by the online conversation history they've had with you, and will make an assumption from that. If you haven't spoken or met in person, the other parties will almost always lean toward the worst-case scenario and assume you are unhappy about the situation. In many cases, they will try to resolve the issue with the least amount of conflict possible, which usually means they will try to lower the price or add something extra to make you happy. Do you see how misinterpretation can cause challenges when verbal and visual cues are missing? This happens with email, through social media, messaging, and texting.

Since communicating non-verbally (online chats, text messaging, email) has become the norm, it's important for all of us to learn strategies that apply to increase our advantages and decrease disadvantages.

Chapter 3

Reasons People
Don't Use the Secret Door

As with anything in life, we all have a fear of the unknown. Our lack of understanding can lead us to confusion or misinterpretation. The only way to get past a fear of the unknown is to make it known. Until then, we live lesser lives, letting our fears have control over us. Let's go over the most common fears people have when it comes to opening the secret door.

1. **Fear of failure** – In every aspect of life, one of the main reasons people don't do something is fear of failure. It's a fear that you will be rejected, that you will fall flat on your face. What's important to understand is that there is no success unless you fail. No one has ever walked through life with all wins. It doesn't work that way. The only way a person learns is through trial and error. You can prepare as much as you want, but guess what, we are all human and we ALL make mistakes. Before you can achieve any greatness in this world or any level of accomplishment, you will fail at some point. What's important is how you handle it. Ask yourself how you handle failure. Do you try to avoid situations where you might fail, or do you look at those situations as opportunities? It seems to me that most people fall somewhere in the middle, if not more towards the avoidance area. All the techniques in this book have helped me experience a lot less failure. Believe they'll do the same for you! And believe in yourself. Believe that when you do fail, you know you will get back up and try

again until you do it right. There is nothing wrong with this. It's the road less traveled, as they say. And good things will come to those who travel that road.

2. **Fear of rejection** – Another thing that may happen when trying these techniques is rejection. Again, this is part of the game. Rejection will happen. They say in the insurance industry there was an old wives' tale that when a claim is filed it is company policy to reject it first and then let the customer fight back to prove that the claim is real. In my personal experience, I'm not sure that is too far from the truth! Remember, much of what we do is based on numbers. Reach out to many people within an organization to stack the odds in your favor that someone will respond. In many cases, your rejection may come in the form of a cyber cold shoulder. This is where the person on the other end simply doesn't reply or your message gets caught in a spam filter. This is one of the reasons I suggest messaging through social networks such as LinkedIn or Facebook. When you are in someone's network, there is a very good chance that your message will at least be seen by your recipient.

3. **Fear of intimidation** – The world is filled with horror stories of how people have been intimidated online or by so-called customer service representatives. No one likes to be intimidated or shamed by someone who purports to be more knowledgeable. I've heard of customer service people being rude to customers and talking down to them. They may say or email something such as, "Didn't you read the warranty information?" Or, "our warranty information clearly states you can't do that." To the average person, this might be extremely uncomfortable. No one likes to feel like that, right? Once you're aware that you're on the receiving

end of a negotiating strategy, you might feel differently. The other party is trying to put you on the defensive so they can get away with giving you less than what you want.

Think about what a trial lawyer does. Their goal is to get witnesses against them to cave in. If you're ever in a situation where someone is trying to intimidate you, know that it's nothing more than a strategy they're using because they fear losing. Stand your ground and keep your goal in mind.

4. **Fear of success**-Yes, fear of success is real. This is basically the fear of wondering what happens if you do become successful. The unknown wonder of "what happens if I do get this job" or "what if I do get what I want out of this negotiation" can stop people in their tracks. They wonder, "Will it add new responsibilities?" "Will I need to do more?" "Now that I have a new car, what happens if I get in an accident?" "What should I do with the extra money I get from this claim? How should I invest it?" The *average* person just wants to be comfortable. They are fine keeping their same lifestyle every day and feeling productive. Any additional thing that might change the norm might cause extra worry or concern and might be a cause for reluctancy in making decisions. Just be aware of this and understand it is very real.

5. **Fear of physical harm**–Most of us would rather avoid confrontation than face it head on. This goes for physical harm as well. When you are negotiating with others, keep in mind that the person on the other end of the email or online correspondence is most likely an employee and just wants to get your issue settled and move on to the next. Don't be afraid to put on your big boy or big girl pants and ask for what you want. You have NOTHING to lose. No

one is going to reach through the computer and slap you around. In most cases those you are negotiating with are thousands of miles away. No one is going to look up your address and pay a visit to you if you are assertive with them. They just want to do their job and get home to their families.

When was the last time you heard of a vendor going after a customer for trying to negotiate with them? NEVER! So just leave it at that. You are the customer. You are in charge in any negotiation. If you are too assertive for a customer service representative, chances are they will suggest you speak with someone else, perhaps higher up in the organization. There's no fear of recourse involved in negotiations when you're the customer.

Chapter 4

Know What You Want

Before making any request, you must first decide what it is that you want. This may seem obvious, but please think carefully about this. When you get into a situation where someone on the other end of your communication is asking you, "So what do you want?", what would you say? You need to know the answer to that question before reaching out.

If you don't, you're leaving yourself open to getting whatever they offer. You don't want to say, "Well, I'm not sure. What can I get?" The negotiator on the other side will offer you the least of what's available.

Imagine an archer trying to hit a bullseye without knowing where the target is? It's not going to happen. So then why should you go into a negotiation not knowing what you want? When you do you are leaving yourself open to their terms and it puts them in control of the negotiation. Now there are occasions where you need to go freestyle and play it by ear because you don't know exactly what is available, but those occasions will be rare.

Decide what the minimum acceptable result would be. Then, leave yourself open to receiving something more, or something different that might prove to be even better than your original thought.

You wouldn't start a trip without a roadmap or GPS, would you? Going into a negotiation without a plan is the same thing. Know your desired outcome before you start. Lay out your roadmap.

Let's use an example where you're a consumer who feels you've been wronged by a company whose services you use. You're ultimately seeking to get what you paid for. To have things put right or the job completed well. You need a repair or replacement. What do you do?

First, you must know what you want, before you reach out to get your situation resolved. Let's say a landscaper runs over one of your favorite rose bushes in your front yard and puts a big rut in your grass. You have several options here. You could ask to have the rosebush replaced and the yard fixed. Or you might want a year's worth of free lawn maintenance, or just an admission of wrongdoing and apology. (Believe it or not, sometimes that one is the hardest to get!) Whatever the case may be, if you don't know what you want going into the negotiation, it's like going into a football game without a play book or trying to bake a cake without a recipe or build a house without blueprints. It's just not going to end well.

If you don't know what you want, your opponent (the person on the other end of the negotiation or customer service rep) will be in control. You may have to take whatever they offer you, and it's not likely to be ideal—at least for you. Most likely it will be to the advantage of your opponent. However, when you start the negotiation knowing what you want, you will have the other person on their heels. Whatever the case is, always remember, nothing is impossible, and if they balk at your initial request you can always negotiate down. It is very difficult to negotiate up!

Get It in Writing

When negotiating verbally, be sure to take accurate notes of the conversation, including notations of the dates of conversations and the names of all parties involved. When negotiating via email or chat your questions and agreements are already in writing so to speak with no chance of going back and saying, "Well, I didn't say that" or "that's not what I meant." Online correspondence is eternal and can be traced back to the exact date and time you typed and sent it.

Having the negotiation in writing works to the advantage of both sides. If you are negotiating an agreement with someone and they send you an offer, it is just as verifiable and traceable as what you send. Keep this in mind when negotiating. Don't accept or offer anything in an email or chat unless you are 100% confident that it is exactly what you want from your negotiation.

When the Initial Offer Isn't What You Want

Whether you're negotiating a purchase, a customer service issue or a request, you'll want to know how to use some effective techniques. One effective way to negotiate is called *the flinch technique*. The flinch technique when used in person is as simple as breathing in quickly, with your teeth clenched and slightly exposed. Typically, you would also frown slightly. You would then say, "Wow, that's more than I really wanted to spend." Or, "Wow, that's not what I expected at all." After that statement, you don't say a word. Be patient and wait for the other person to break the silence. The onus will be on them to make the next move.

If this is a situation where you're buying something, know that salespeople often have leeway in adjusting the prices on their wares. Wait them out and they will often drop the price. I have gotten as much as half off the initial price of a large ticket item by using this technique. That's right, half off!

This strategy works online as well. You just eliminate the body language. Instead of flinching in person, you can email something like, "Oh, that seems more than we want to spend", or "Wow, we didn't realize that was going to be that expensive." And then just wait for an answer. Don't add anything else to your message such as trying to explain why you think it's too much. The flinch works best when it is simple, to the point, and no communication occurs after the statement until the other side replies.

The other parties to the message know nothing more than that the amount is more than you wanted to spend. They can't read your body language. They don't know if you're comparing them to the competition, or looking for an entirely different product. Since they don't know, most people will err on the side of caution and assume they're losing the sale. As we discussed earlier, they will then try to resolve the issue, or save the sale, by dropping the price or adding something of value if you go ahead.

Some sales pros will send back a broad, vague counteroffer that leaves you open to further negotiating techniques. Or, they may ask more questions. With email negotiations time is on your side. Every minute, hour or day that you wait to answer, allows the person on the other end of the conversation to think. About what? Well, about what you are thinking. They'll be asking themselves, "What might I have done better to make this deal run smoothly?" Or it might be something like "Is that person still interested?" The longer you wait to respond, the more your opponent will be thinking about the situation. Keep that in mind the next time you are in negotiation with someone online. Time is on *your* side. Not *theirs*.

Just don't wait too long to respond. If your salesperson sends a second or third follow up email, it's best not to leave them hanging too long. They'll assume the sale is lost and move on to working with someone else. This will make it more difficult for you to pick up the negotiation later. You want to respond enough to let them know you're interested, but hold back from making an agreement until you get the offer or concessions you really want.

Add-Ons and Upgrades

Add-ons or upgrades are usually used at the end of a negotiation, when all major points of a deal have been agreed to. These are used as a final nibble negotiation that gives you just a bit more. Let's say that you are negotiating with a manufacturer to replace a small appliance. In most cases, even though the appliance may be covered under a warranty, the shipping is not. If shipping *is* included, it's often via the slowest, cheapest means possible. As long as it hasn't been brought up before this point, email something like this: "That does include free overnight shipping, correct?" Nine times out of 10, if done diplomatically and in a timely manner, the manufacturer will concede to free overnight shipping or at least free standard shipping, especially if it was an involved negotiation.

Bed Accessory Example

About two years ago my wife and I purchased a new hybrid bed and, for about the first six months, it was awesome. Around then we discovered a malfunction. I emailed the manufacturer, pointing out their 15-year warranty, and asked if they could replace the part that was faulty. They agreed to do it. A few weeks went by, and after a few more contacts with our representative, we finally had their service group come out.

At the time we thought nothing more about it. Then we received a follow up phone call from the company. The person on the other end of the line said, since we had such a problem, we could pick any product from the bedding section of the website and they would send it to us at no charge. They suggested a pillow or a set of sheets. Simple enough, right?

However, a good negotiator never just jumps into a negotiation blind. Nor does he or she usually accept the first offer. No, a good negotiator gathers all the facts and then takes action knowing exactly what he wants. I said I would call the rep back at a later date because I would like to take some time to look things over with my wife. The rep agreed and we said our goodbyes.

My wife and I looked through the website and noticed they had a dual temperature comforter in the bedding section of their website - $2,900 retail. By the way, we paid $2,300 for the whole bed. Remember, they said, "Any item in the bedding section online."

I mustered up the courage to call back the rep and told her in a very casual, matter-of-fact way, we would like the dual temp comforter as our free bedding gift. Now deep down, I knew this wasn't what they were talking about when they said, "any bedding item." However, this was testing the water.

As you can imagine, the representative came across offended and actually said the words "Nice Try." (Not the best customer service by any means!) So, in a very polite way I continued to explain that when you click on bedding section on their website all these items popped up, so I just assumed these were bedding items. The person on the other end of the phone began to get very belligerent and said, "You can't honestly think we are going to give you an item that cost more than your bed, do you?"

Now, the thing to remember here is to not let your emotions get the best of you. Every part of me wanted to reach across the phone line and shred this person verbally into 1,000 pieces. And you might have felt that way as well. But really, what would you have achieved? You would have won your argument, ruined another person's day and made them feel bad, and have absolutely nothing but a waste of an hour of your time. That doesn't sound like a win at all. So, what should you do in a situation like this? Step back. Take a breath. Regroup.

I said in a calm voice, "Well, I can appreciate what you're saying, and I am sorry for the misunderstanding here. However, you can see how this might be misleading, right?" Then I waited. After a pause on the phone, the rep said, "Yes, I guess I can. We are only allowed to give up to 15% of your original purchase price as a gift." BINGO. That is what I was waiting for! Now, I knew what I had to work with. So, I politely said, "Can you send me an email stating that for my records?" (Really, I wanted more to make sure this was in THEIR records.) My wife and I then picked out a $200 version of a dual comfort warmer and with a little proof of our conversation, it was ordered with free shipping!

With one hour of negotiating and a little patience, I got us really exactly what we really wanted. This can be done with almost anything in any situation online or on the phone. You just need to know what you want, who the right person is to give it to you, and in this case, what they are permitted to give you. Oh yeah, and keep your emotions out of it!

Extras, Extras!

Going back to the topic of knowing what you want, here are a few examples of extras I've negotiated for over the years:

- Free tire rotation with the purchase of new brakes

- Free stain remover for new carpeting or furniture

- Furniture polish added to the purchase of a new coffee table

- Free lifetime oil change with a tune up

- Free lifetime car wash with the purchase of a car

- Free extended warranty with the purchase of a new car or large ticket item

- Free furnace filters with duct cleaning

- Free trimming of other trees with a tree removal

- Free country club membership for new executive hire

- Setup for a new home entertainment system or anything big and complex

- Free bottle of champagne with the purchase of a limo ride

- Free delivery on almost anything

- Free birthday treat or appetizer at a restaurant

- Free upgraded hotel room

- Additional fertilizer application or aeration treatment with the purchase of a full year landscape package

Be creative and think of things before the negotiation that won't be out of reach, yet will help to sweeten the deal to make you a life-long customer. The best time to request these extras is right before you commit to payment. (The moment of truth, if you will!) In many cases, there is a secret treat or lever the salesperson can pull that is only given to friends, family members, and life-long users of the secret door techniques!

Chapter 5

Resolving Service Issues

How many times have you had a problem with a plumber or service person and just couldn't get things right? You may have tried to reach out to someone online only to find there that no one responds to your requests. Or, when you do reach someone, they don't seem to understand what the issue is or how to resolve it. You may hear the tried-and-true "company policy" line from them. Or, worse, have them listen to your complaint but offer no solution at all.

I'm pretty sure everyone has encountered the communication-killing phone tree when trying to get something resolved. You get lost in a labyrinth of phone prompts that lead only to voice mail for someone who is not identified other than "You've reached Sally, please leave me a message." You don't even know if Sally still works at the company, if she has the responsibility or power to deal with your complaint or will listen to your message any time within the next week because she's out of the office or on vacation.

Well I'm here to tell you, there are many ways beyond the customer service line to get what you want when you have been serviced poorly. Here is a real-life story of how I got my washing machine repaired using the secret online door:

A while back, we had a problem with our washing machine. For some odd reason, it would not get out of rinse mode. When it hit that area in the wash cycle, it would get stuck in the "fill" mode. Even if I shut the machine off, it kept filling up with water. Want to talk about scary! I had to literally shut the water off to the machine to get it to stop. So, I contacted the appliance store where I purchased the machine and asked for a service person to come out and fix it. My goal at the time was to get my washing machine fixed as fast as possible.

With two college kids living at home, this was critical. I was told it would be two weeks before they could get someone out. That was bad enough. Then, the service rep who showed up admitted to having no experience working with appliances—that his expertise was home theater! He did four hours of testing on the machine, and of course could not find anything wrong with it. He ended up cleaning it out and saying the issue was because we added too much soap to the wash.

My wife and I scratched our heads over that one. We paid the $150 service fee and tried the machine again. It did work better for about a week. Then, we had the same problem. So, this time, a bit more irritated, back on the phone I went with the same company and explained the problem. They apologized and said the soonest that they could get somebody out was two weeks later. Once the problem was found, it might take another week to get parts in and those parts might cost a couple hundred dollars. What a pain, right?

I pleaded with them to see if I could move the appointment up, but all they could say was that they were going to try to escalate the request. This was the tipping point for me, so I turned to the secret door. I went on LinkedIn and found the vice president of customer service for the entire company and sent the following InMail message to him.

> Dear (Name of V.P.), I had a service call about 3-4 weeks ago on our washer because it was stuck in the rinse cycle and the only way to stop it was to cut the water to the unit. It took over two weeks to get someone out here initially. At the time they said to me "they don't work on washers very often" and came to the conclusion "we put too much soap in our wash." Now weeks later, we are having the same issue. They again pushed our service call out two weeks. Not very good public relations, wouldn't you say? Can you please see if you can light a fire somewhere to get someone out sooner that knows what they are talking about? Here is the work order: 42466410

Sincerely, Dan Portik Owner/President
http://www.Bvsfilmproductions.com Avon, Ohio 440-653-9911

I received confirmation that he received my message.

His response was on the same day.

Dan, thanks for reaching out. I am following up with our teams on this.

4:46 PM

Well, using this method could not have worked any faster. I received a call the next day from the regional manager of the service department of the store, and he asked if someone could stop out in an hour (or less) to fix the issue! An hour? I said I take it you received a call from the vice president. He said yes and apologized as if his job was on the line. I said, "I didn't mean to pull rank but almost 1 month without a working washing machine was unacceptable." More apologies were given, and we hung up.

The story gets even better. This time the guy that came out within an hour of the phone call ran about an hour of tests. After I showed him what was happening, he said it was a water pressure switch valve. He went on to say. "You can order this through us and there will be a $150 trip charge and one hour of labor at $55 as well as a part charge of around $50. Or you can go on eBay and grab one for around $15, take two screws off here and here to get the top off and one screw and one hose here and put the top back on and it will be fixed." Ah, I said, "You rock," and he left me with his card and *personal cell number*. I immediately went online and discovered that the guy lied to me. He said the part would be $15.00. I found it for $13.94! I received it within days and got the washer running just fine. And now I have a tech's personal mobile number and he is very aware that I know his boss's boss! That relationship is invaluable. I have put his number on speed dial in my phone for any further issues.

When we unpack what happened here, there are a few things that make this an extremely effective technique.

1. There needs to be a legitimate claim. This means that there is something faulty or someone that has done you wrong within an organization that can be proven beyond a "he said/she said" accusation. If I were to have contacted the vice president after my initial issue, there would have been a good chance he may not have returned my InMail or may have said I'll see what I can do. But the fact that I had several compounded issues, intensified the concern and issue with their company.

2. I made sure my company name and title were on the InMail. Even if he didn't look up my profile online, my credentials looked professional and in order.

3. My message, for the most part, stayed professional and to the point. I made it easy for him to look up the order by leaving an order number.

I follow up with two last steps in this negotiation. First, I successfully replaced the part and ensured the washer was fixed. Then, I contacted the vice president one last time to apologize for being a bit abrupt with him and thank him for personally getting the problem resolved. I let him know his team did a great job and mentioned the tech's name.

I felt good about how this ended up being resolved and took steps to ensure that everyone else did, too. An over-the-top victory in any negotiation is when everyone walks away feeling good about themselves, each other, and the final outcome.

Never underestimate the power of the secret door. The end of this story is that I received a follow-up call from the regional manager of the company, who gave me his personal contact information and informed me that my message made it to the CEO of the company. I'm guessing my issue will be used as a lesson for future customer service strategies. And, when I reach out for another service issue, I know my name is flagged in their computer to receive escalated service.

How do I know that? Approximately one month after the washer incident, we had an issue with our stove that we purchased from the same company. There were some scratches and slight build-up on the glass top burners. The stove was still under warranty. My wife had mentioned it to me on several occasions and complained that it just wasn't coming clean—no matter what we did. She kept saying it was ruined and nothing could be done about it, because she read the warranty, and this was not covered by it.

Truthfully, I really didn't think anything of it. To me it looked like something we might be able to live with. But then again, I'm a guy and most of us could eat cold beans out of a can and it would be okay, right? However, my wife felt a little differently about the issue. She was convinced this wouldn't be covered under warranty and there was nothing that could be done. So, I said to my wife, "What do we have to lose by calling and finding out what could be done?" She was not optimistic at all about the situation at the time. I called the number on the extended service contract that we had and, surprisingly, it just so happened to be to the same repair service that fixed the washer. I simply told them my name and mentioned my problem.

To be very candid with you, this was a very gray area in their warranty. From what we saw, it read that the burners needed to be not working to have the glass top replaced. However, before I could say a word, the person on the other end of the phone asked me if Wednesday of the following week would be a good day to have a tech come out and replace the top. *Replace the entire top? Really?* This seemed too good to be true. But guess what, I'm in the computer. My name, my records and all my history with that company are right there, including involvement by higher-ups in the company. Could this be a coincidence that they bent all the rules and ordered a brand new, glass burner top with no questions asked? My guess is that in the records, the name of that higher-up made a difference. For all they know, he might be a good friend or relative of mine. And with that in mind, the voice on the other end of the phone wanted nothing to do with giving me a hard time in any way. All I can say is that was cool! Life as a customer is so much easier when you're in the system. Not to mention, I earned a really big kiss from my better half!

Beware here that your name is not flagged for a negative reason. Only reach out for legitimate problems with products. If you return too many things to some companies, you can, in some cases, be marked as a habitual returner. This is somebody that uses a product for a while and then when the warranty is almost up somehow seems to have the product broken and they will return it for another one.

There is a department store that marked me as a habitual returner because I returned four items in one month! I'm sure this can be a problem in the big-box do-it-yourself stores where someone brings an item back after using it for a project. In my situation, I had very reasonable issues, ranging from grills not working right to broken rake handles. Remember, the higher up you go online and the more secret doors you use, the quicker these issues can go away.

When the Secret Door is Not Necessary

Sometimes using the secret door is not necessary if you use some simple techniques when dealing with the first level of customer service representative. If you are working with a representative and you come to an agreement on the next steps of a negotiation, or if there is a follow up on an order, always try to get their full name and way that you and their supervisor can reach out to them. I always found it best to see if they can send an email to me recapping exactly what was discussed, and what the next steps are for whom.

If none of the above can be given to you, ask them to give you their employee identification number or the case number. This can be used to your advantage because you will have a way of tracing the issue and promises back to that person. This assigns accountability to the person you are dealing with. This can be a strong motivator when getting something accomplished and avoid having to travel any further up the chain of command.

Another way to head off a trip to the secret door is to get to know your customer service rep on the other end of your communication. Have you ever heard the expression, keep your friends close to you but keep your enemies even closer? So when you are trying to get a problem resolved with whomever you are dealing with, it is not so easy for them to treat you like just another problem customer if they know a little about you, other than you are a complaining person on the other end of the conversation. That said, get to know your CSR, ask them where they are located or what's the weather like there. I have always found it fascinating when I talk about the snow in Ohio to someone in India that has never seen or felt snow. They can't comprehend what it would be like to shovel a foot of snow out of your driveway before you pull out. Or when we talk about the cost of education in other countries. I always learn something new.

For instance, when I spoke to one of the young ladies on the other end of the phone from India about school. I found out that a four-year college education was a fraction of the cost of one in the United States. These are great conversation topics to start a slightly more personal conversation, to get on a different level with your rep while they are looking up information for you. You will be surprised what a little small talk will do to get you on a different level of help.

Using the customer service representative's name during conversations is also helpful. It humanizes the issue. Thanking them for their help is also wise. When you are kind and complimentary you initiate a sense of obligation on the part of the others involved in the resolution to go out of their way to please you.

Chapter 6

Organization Pays

Being organized will help open the secret door wide. My wife and I make a good team. She keeps all the warranty papers in a file cabinet in our spare bedroom (as well as online in electronic format) neatly alphabetized. When I talk with her about something that needs to be fixed through a warranty, she goes to the spare room and takes a picture of the paperwork and sends it to me via text. That way the original never leaves the file. On more than one occasion this has helped to keep my blood pressure down and save hours of aggravation.

If you have someone like my wife, a husband, or significant other to help you with being organized, take advantage of it. However, if you don't, keep all of your warranty paperwork in one place. You don't need an elaborate system, just a single, accessible location where it will all go. Having the warranty paperwork makes things simpler.

However, if you don't have warranty papers, or if you might have lost them, not to worry. I have found by using the secret door, in many cases, the actual warranties mean nothing. What's important is to have all your ducks in a row. If you use all the steps in this book and reach out to the right person, the limitation of your warranty may magically disappear.

Be Clear in Your Messages

Make sure when you send online correspondence that you tell your story in a clear and logical way, so there is no chance of misunderstanding. If there is a product or company that has not performed up to your standards, or if you have been treated poorly by a customer service rep, before you go to the next level, get organized and take all the emotion out of your messaging. There is nothing worse to a higher-up than an email rant that goes on and on, using profanity or belittling someone's company. Keep everything professional and to the point. If it requires you to step back for an hour or even a day before you write anything, take the time to do it. You want to make a positive, professional impression that has impact.

Make a Video of Your Issue

If you have a problem or issue with a product or service, make a video of it and learn how to post it, add it to a message, or store it in the cloud and include a link to it in your messaging. There is absolutely no better way to convey your information than through the use of video.

Videos can be a highly effective and sometimes a brutally honest way of showing the world just exactly how a product works, or doesn't work as well as a company represents it. In some cases, it's like taping a stick of dynamite to the secret door handle and lighting the fuse! Videos of poor customer service tend to go viral. There have been several instances of this in the airline industry. This type of negative attention can have devastating results for a company. People may choose to boycott that business, which in turn impacts employees, stockholders, and possibly an entire industry. Negative videos tend to get attended to quickly once companies become aware of them.

That being said, before you decide to publicly post a video, just send it to someone at the company you are having an issue with. Seek out someone who cares and is capable of giving you what you want. With a video and social media, you always have the option of letting it go public if you need to use it as part of your negotiating tactic. It's not that you would use it as a threat (that could create a legal situation that you would want to avoid), but rather to air your complaint. I don't know about you, but if I ever saw a video of an employee of mine treating a customer poorly, I would feel two things. Angry at myself for not training them properly and slightly fearful as to the negative repercussions that may occur. I'd be contacting you immediately!

Make Yourself Available

There may be times when it's a struggle to reach the right person through the secret door. Sometimes when you travel to the secret door, it is locked, and no one is home. The person may have that familiar online message on their "door" reading "out of office." You will need to be flexible in both approaching them and in being available for them to re-contact you. When attempting to reach someone of stature or public notoriety, their schedule is likely more complicated than yours. It is your responsibility to make sure you are available for the call, chat session, or any other type of correspondence that is likely to occur. You can't dash off an email with a request or challenge, then not check your email for a response until days or weeks later.

Making yourself available shows you have respect for the other person's time and that you are a responsible person. This will help to keep the secret door open until the next time you want to reach out to them. If someone at that high level is late to get back to you, don't let that be a point of contention. Instead use it to open the secret door a little wider. If they fail to keep a promise or commitment, they'll likely feel obligated to do a little bit more for you once you do connect.

Keep in mind, especially if you are dealing with executives, that their schedules may not be carved in stone. Planes can be delayed, traffic can tie them up, and unexpected meetings occur. Sometimes it is best when they reach out to you later than expected or need to cut their times with you short to say, "I completely understand and how about we reschedule at your convenience." It's always wise to stay calm and available during any negotiation. You'll have a better result when you *respond* rather than *react* to any situation. Taking the high road and remaining polite will get you farther than expressing your frustration beyond the issue at hand.

Chapter 7

Social Media's Secret Doors

I'm pretty sure that when most social media platforms got started, they were designed simply to allow people to be "social." The goal was to provide a means of communication and entertainment. Social media platforms are one of the few means of communication whose evolution has been dictated by its users.

Sure, people initially checked out the various platforms to see what they were all about, but then, the ideas for use expanded exponentially. Beyond personal use for sharing, most platforms also include commercial use, educational purposes, sponsored promotions, advertising, and shopping carts. With a little patience and creativity in researching, you can gain access to valuable information and make incredible connections.

Social media can be a wonderful thing, or it can be a terrible thing for companies and individuals. It's a great place to engage customers, gather testimonials, share information and tell them all about the wonderful products and services you offer, as well as drum up business with coupons and special offers. It can also, with the right number of followers, generate income and be used for market research on the launch of a new product or service. However, there is another side that we can use it for. It can be used to get attention to an issue or problem and have action taken. Yes, there is a secret door here as well.

Social media is the only platform of communication where you are not restricted from reaching out to anyone at any time. Unlike email or phone calls, in most cases there are no spam filters or gatekeepers to contend with. It's really a free-for-all of communication. Twitter, LinkedIn, YouTube, or really any place that the company or individual you are dealing with lives and communicates with their target audience, could be a great place to get their attention. This can also be overwhelming. There are thousands of places where your person or company can be hiding. So how do you find them? How do you find the secret door to where they live? It might take some doing—maybe some deep investigating. One of the simplest ways is start clicking around. Check online first to see where they are most prominent and go that direction, to their blog, social network or discussion page. Once you find it, be prepared to state your case.

If you feel you have been wronged, cheated, or treated unfairly in a business or consumer situation, you can use the secret door to bring it up on a company's social media channel or wall. You may think that big companies monitor their social media pages and would never let a bad comment be seen by the public. Believe me, you would be shocked at how many companies don't secure their channels very well. Many are unaware that people are able to post for everyone to see what's on their social sites.

When companies do closely monitor their sites, that's a good thing for consumers. That means someone is seeing all posted information before it goes live. If there is a negative post, it usually gets acted upon pretty darn fast.

YouTube's Money-Saving Opportunities

YouTube has a secret door to find out anything about a product or service you may have a problem with. I sometimes believe that with a small amount of effort, you can find the answers to almost any question using the YouTube secret door.

As a guitarist for almost 40 years, if I want to find out how to play a specific song that I just can't quite figure out, I go to YouTube and search through videos for it. Inevitably there on one of the pages is a teenager playing that exact same song and showing me note by note exactly what to do!

If there is a problem or issue with a product or service, there is a pretty good chance, especially if it is a popular item, that there is somebody online talking about a fix or where you can get something fixed. But keep in mind there are a lot of negative Nellies out there. So, if someone says "I tried to get my car fixed by that company, but the warranty had ended so I just said forget it, I will never buy another car from them" they obviously never read this book.

Let's move on to another technique that we use to get around the warranty issue. Because remember, there is no such thing as being out of warranty when using the secret door. Right?

The Moen Story

Here is an example of a surprise that I received when I tried to replace a faucet. There was a faucet in our upstairs bathroom with an annoying drip that eventually became a small stream. After a brief exercise to try to remove the rusted parts on it, I assumed I was going to need to head to the local hardware store for replacements and pay a plumber to put in two matching faucets. Rather than bearing that expense, I decided to try to remedy the situation myself. I turned to the secret online door for help. Before taking the bad faucet apart I decided to check on YouTube to see if anyone else ever replaced a faucet like mine. Guess what? Someone had! And, they recorded a video about it.

I started playing the video and following the instructions as to how to take my faucet apart. Most of the pieces were rusted and were breaking off before I could even remove them. As I was watching the video, I heard the person say they were working on a Moen faucet and that Moen has a *lifetime warranty* on their products with no questions asked, and he had received the parts necessary to repair his faucet at no charge.

Armed with this information, I asked myself, "Could I happen to have a Moen faucet here?" So, I put on my glasses and looked at the little sticker on the front of the faucet. And sure enough, it was a Moen. I felt like I had just received a "get out of jail free" card! I reached out to Moen through their customer service web page. They needed a photo of the faucet and some details. Once they confirmed the faucet was theirs, they agreed to ship the replacement parts.

You can learn almost anything on YouTube, including how to repair items in your home. Many licensed contractors even offer the lessons. Of course, they're hoping that when you run into larger issues, you'll call them, but there's a ton you can learn to do on your own!

Facebook's Secret Door

Facebook's secret door can be found on every company's Facebook page. Not only will you see promotions from those companies but questions from consumers and their answers. It can be a great opportunity to research any issues you're having with that company's products or services.

I would use the Company Page on Facebook somewhere between trying to reach their customer service department, and going directly to a higher-up in person. You may find other people with the same problem or issue on the wall of their page. A simple resolution might already be covered there. A comment may have been made naming a specific person or department who was especially helpful.

I would also use this secret door to reach out to the people who are posting on the company's Facebook page. With direct contact, they might supply you with a confidential link or number that was not meant to be seen by the public. They might offer a simple fix when you thought there was a missing part while putting your son's new bike together that you just bought from that company, when in reality that part was only available for the deluxe model.

Keep in mind before you post a comment or complaint on a company's Facebook page to give a true, clear and honest representation of your situation. Make sure it can be defended and backed up by facts. Don't embellish or blow out of proportion what has been done to you. And always document your issue with pictures or video.

Not that it's likely to happen with every complaint, but there is nothing stopping a company from putting a lawyer on it if they feel they are losing business because of your post. In my opinion, that is just super bad business to do so, and 99.9% of the time you will just get a call or email from a customer service representative, to try and solve the problem with the least amount of exposure possible. Nearly every successful company's upper management, up to the CEO, knows the value of a happy customer. Just remember to play fair. You can get what you want without damaging their business.

My Facebook Video Story

Once upon a time I had a lawn service company that forgot what the term "service" meant. There were big patches in my lawn where they couldn't keep the grass growing. Not being a fan of large brown patches, I tried time and time again to call and even corner the technician to ask about it. No one would follow up or help me in any way. However, at the first of the month they would always remember to debit my checking account for their monthly fee.

Needless to say, you can imagine my frustration with the situation. So, I decided to take matters into my own hands. I went out to my front yard and recorded a video of the areas of dead grass and then posted them on the company's Facebook page with a request for assistance. By the way, this was a large, national company I was dealing with.

Within an hour of posting my message of dissatisfaction and the video of my yard, I received a call from their corporate office apologizing for the issues that I had and promising they would be resolved. Within a few days, I had a district manager come out to look at my yard. I was told they would take care of it immediately. A few days later, an angry supervisor came out late at night and tried to fix the problems in my yard. When I tried to speak with him, I only got one-word answers as if his job was on the line. It was pretty uncomfortable, and his attitude did not reflect a caring customer service person in any way. What he did still didn't resolve the issue. I had to contact them a third time. (Three strikes and you're out?!)

What I decided was that sometimes you don't get the best result and you need to know when to let go. So even though the secret door worked for getting the attention of the national lawn maintenance company, I realized part of the problem went deeper in the organization. They had a culture problem in that none of their people acted as if customer service was of value. They never followed up again and never did fix my yard problems. I fired them and hired another group to handle it.

I guess the moral of the story in that case was that there's only so much we can expect and so much time that's worth putting into reaching people. We can't fix the basic psychology of some vendors. In this case, they just didn't care about delivering quality service on any level. By the way, I still get calls from salespeople and mail solicitations from that company, on a monthly basis, telling me how great their company is and asking if I would like to join up with their lawn service to receive great pricing and outstanding service. I feel bad for their persistent sales and marketing teams in that they probably have to work three times as hard as the competition to get and keep clients, due to poor delivery.

Want to Reach a Rock Star?

I have a friend who owns a small recording studio. Almost every night he converses with some of the biggest rock stars in the world on Facebook messenger about the latest audio gear, songs they wrote and the reasons they wrote them. Those rock stars are often in a hotel room on tour, at their homes, or some exotic location.

One day, my friend decided to use the secret door to get something more out of those relationships. He has a small charity that records a Christmas CD every year, so he reached out to a very famous singer through Facebook and asked if he would do a song for the next year's CD. And guess what? He said yes! If my friend had followed normal channels of reaching out, he may have been stopped by a gatekeeper. His message may never have gotten directly to the rock star.

In the world of recording, musicians no longer need to be in the studio to record. They can be 10,000 miles away, receive the audio files and record the vocals on their computers and send them in to an audio engineer. With the internet and social media platforms the world has become smaller than ever. We can work simply with everyone at any time! Follow the advice in this book and use the ingredients in the right order, and there is no one you can't reach or anything you cannot achieve.

LinkedIn's Secret Door

Earlier in this book we talked about knowing what you want before you begin to negotiate or attempt to use the secret door. Well, there is one more ingredient to this equation. You must reach out to someone who is capable of giving you what you want. If the social media secret door won't open for you, it may be time for you to use what I call "The Higher Up" secret door. This door by far has been the most effective for me personally for many years, to reach and get more than what I have wanted or needed. This secret door is found on LinkedIn.

LinkedIn is a place where you can reach business professionals through a tool called "InMail." It's not likely you will find your favorite celebrities on LinkedIn. However, those who are employed by celebrities are likely to have profiles there.

So how can an InMail help you through the secret door? Well, when it comes to complaints or negotiations, you will find higher ups in companies readily accessible. And, some will be quite surprised when you send them an InMail through LinkedIn with a complaint attached to it. In the subject line, put "customer complaint" or "disappointed in your company's service or product" and you may be surprised about the response you get and from whom.

Some vice presidents or regional managers of companies never get a chance to see a complaint firsthand. Most really care about customer service in their firms and will listen and respond. They are more likely to understand how the success customers have with their products impacts the bottom line of the organization. (It could also impact their salaries or bonuses!)

When You Have a Name, Search for an Address

Even if you don't hear directly from a higher-up you reach out to, once you have their contact information, consider returning a defective item directly to them, rather than to the warehouse or customer service department. I've used this technique with very positive results.

Once upon a time, I purchased a higher-end wireless headset. The cost was around $200. I used it for about two years and some of the pieces broke on it. I thought nothing of it, put it in a box and stored it away, thinking someday I would fix it or send it back. Three or four more years went by and I forgot about it. I ended up buying a newer headset from the same manufacturer for around the same price. I used it for about two years and it then stopped working.

At this point, it dawned on me that this was the second unit I purchased over a 6-year span that broke. Now, I was on a mission. I dug through my old storage boxes and found the first unit. I took it as well as the newer unit, packed them both up in a box and sent them both back, FedEx signature required, to one of the vice presidents of customer service for the company. I included a letter similar to this one.

Dear (V.P. first name)

I am writing to express my dissatisfaction with your company's headsets. Over the past 6 years I have purchased two of your units and both of them have broken and fallen apart. I have always known (manufactures name) to be associated with the highest quality products. With this in mind, I would like to know what can be done to keep me as a life-long customer.

Sincerely

Dan Portik

About a week went by and I received a call and an email from an escalation executive, saying she received my package and was very sorry for the issues that I was having. They reviewed all of the contents in the package I sent back and wanted to offer me their top-of-the-line Bluetooth head set at no charge. The retail value was $799. They just needed to confirm my address to ship it. Cool, huh?

Like I said, I have done this on several occasions and have yet to have it backfire. Receiving a package like that is somewhat of a shock factor to them. To make this work successfully, you must make sure you do the research throughly either on LinkedIn or Google to find out to whom and where to send your item back. If you are sending it to a corporate headquarters in Minnesota, but your vice president is a regional guy and works out of the State of Washington, your package may take months to get to your contact, if at all. But rest assured, this approach is impactful. Next, make sure the letter you send is to the point, not negative in any way. Be complimentary in some sense (i.e., "I've always known your products to be high-quality."). Express hope for a resolution with a call to action or reward for the vendor (keeping you as a long-term client).

Many higher-ups will reach out to you directly. Others may assign an assistant or customer service manager to help you. When they receive such an assignment from a higher up, they are extremely attentive to your needs and will try to do almost anything to help you out. Why? Because their boss's boss told them to do so.

I have found that about 50% of the time that I have reached out through LinkedIn's secret door, I receive a response to my InMail from exactly whom I was trying to contact. Usually they will be very apologetic and will say "they will look into it or have someone on their staff look into it for them." Keep in mind, now you have an executive who has put in writing that someone will look into it for you. There is something about the fact it is in writing that gives it legs much faster than if you were told that verbally.

Here's my take on this. In my own case, if a customer sends an email with a complaint, I now have a quick and verifiable way of sending this complaint to the proper person in my organization to put the responsibility directly on that next person down the line to get it handled. Think about it, with a push of a forward button and/or a CC and typing one line, the burden is off my shoulders and put squarely on the shoulders of someone else in my company. That person may be in a better position than I am to get this handled, but the customer still has my name as a contact person so I'm still "on the hook" for a resolution.

If I ever hear back from that customer with the same complaint, I know exactly where to turn to find out why their issue was not resolved to the customer's liking and, adversely, so does the person on the other end of that CC or forward, which makes it that much more important to all parties involved to get this handled. Online messaging, what a wonderful thing—for us as consumers and the executives you reach! I recommend using this door sparingly, only when needed, and watching what kind of results you get. It can be pretty amazing!

Chapter 8

Nothing is Ever Out of Warranty or Too Big to Ask

Nearly every product in the world offers some type of warranty. Most are quite limited. However, in my experience nothing is ever out of warranty when you use the secret online door to reach out.

Like in the Moen plumbing company, which was discussed earlier in the book. With my most recent contact, I just snapped a picture of my faucet. When it was determined they no longer had parts for my model, Moen offered to send me a compatible faucet, or I could go to their website and get credit for that faucet's value and choose whatever I wanted. Well, of course I picked a much nicer, more expensive faucet. I won as a consumer and Moen has won a customer for life. I would never think of buying plumbing supplies from another vendor, even if they were considerably less expensive.

More and more businesses are now taking the attitude of "no questions asked" when it comes to returns. Why? Because the average person will buy a product and if it doesn't work as expected, they will put it aside and say, "I'll take it back next week." And we all know that next week always stays in next week land. Most people just won't follow through and return items. Those that do remain loyal customers, because there's no hassle in doing so. So by a company offering a "no questions asked" return policy, they retain a more loyal customer base which far outweighs the returns that are brought back.

As a rule, most companies create warranties to make the general populace feel good that their products will be free from defects in workmanship, and that the company will stand behind them if there are issues. Beyond that "workmanship" definition, most companies do not offer a lot of help. For 99 percent of people that's just fine. Why? Because that's what they've come to expect. Like sheep, most people follow the commands of the sheepherder—in this case, the company "policies."

Those policies and limited warranties are, in essence, fences put between us and them when it comes to customer service. In reality, the boundaries created are only in our minds. The limitations created by warranties are for the other guys, not for you and me and others who understand the methods for using secret online doors. We look beyond written limitations to what companies really want—loyal, happy customers who buy their products over and over again and recommend those products to others.

When the Warranty Runs Out

How many times have you had a product perform just fine until about a month or two after the warranty expires? It's almost as if there's a timer built into some products to implode at the warranty date. By using the strategies in this book, it's simple to transform those outdated warranties into unlimited, lifetime warranties.

Think about it. Companies want to earn profits, of course. However, most executive teams know that the way to earn those profits is by putting out quality products at fair prices, then standing behind those products to keep the customers happy. When it comes to warranty issues, most would rather lose a warranty and keep the customer over doing the opposite. That just makes sense, doesn't it?

Sadly, the people in many organizations who feel that way are not the customer service representatives. They're the higher-ups we've talked about, or executives whose income and lifestyle might be impacted by unhappy customers who purchase from the competition and encourage their friends to do the same. Those are the people you want to reach if you're not satisfied with the results you got from customer service. Most customer service representatives are more worried about getting in trouble, or possibly losing their jobs by over-extending the warranty, than they are with keeping customers happy. That tends to be a cultural issue within organizations. You are less likely to run into challenges with those companies that put the emphasis on customer satisfaction from the top down.

Getting a Year-Old Laptop Replaced for One Worth Four Times as Much

I little while back, I tried to buy a computer online from one of the major computer manufacturers. I needed to fix some issues with an existing laptop and purchase a workstation for one of our editing suites. I began by emailing the representative that I have used in the past when ordering. She had been very detailed and helpful in the past. I sent several emails to her using an email address from the past but didn't receive a response from her. After two weeks, I tried again thinking that for some reason my message may have gotten caught in her spam folder. As it turned out, that's exactly what happened. She returned my message, apologizing for the delay. She had been promoted and was now using a different email address. Messages forwarded from her previous address were not always going through.

She continued to explain that with the new promotion, she was no longer able to service my account. She offered to send me to an assistant in another area that would be able to assist me. When contacted, the new representative told me she was in the middle of handling a very large sale and wouldn't be able to handle my request immediately. Hmm?!

I went to work using my secret door strategies. After about two months of searching and making connections, I reached the right vice president of the company through LinkedIn. After explaining my issue, I was able to get an escalation team of no less than four people assigned to my account. At the time, I said to myself, "Wow, it worked again!"

Now, you would think with four people, we could get things done effectively and quickly. Not necessarily. Now, I had four people, all not knowing what the other's responsibility was, not communicating with each other and thinking one of the others was handling things. Each of them had expressed eagerness to help because a higher-up told them to, but not one took ownership of the problem.

At the time of the writing of this book, I have four issues I am dealing with regarding computers I need fixed or have been trying to order, and only one issue has been addressed. One issue is the purchase of a laptop that was shipped, but not to my specifications. It's hard knowing that so many of my issues should have been fixed within a few days. Had someone taken charge of this situation, I would have purchased two new laptops by now, too. Granted, I'm not a large client like some corporations who purchase hundreds of laptops every year, but I'm still a customer with long-term value to the company.

Believing that I had to address one problem at a time, I chose the issues I'd be having with my laptop for over a year. The issues ranged from software not loading to the display screen not working. I chose to reach out to the person I felt would be best to handle just that issue and ask for the impossible. I asked for the company to take my laptop back (one that I'd been using for over a year), and replace it, for the same price, with the best computer they had. The model I asked for specifically was valued at four-times what I had paid for mine.

I covered all my bases. I knew the person I was asking this of had been told by their boss to make me happy. It took about two weeks, but the paperwork for my request was put through. I was able to return my year-old computer at 100 percent credit. The representatives told me to pick out whatever laptop I wanted. So, I went online and picked the most expensive one with the most memory they had. The rep got back to me and said they couldn't do an exact exchange for my year-old computer. However, they could go as low as their cost, which was 50 percent off the new computer. So instead of $5000, they would sell it to me for $2,500.

I kept asking for upgrades, additions and further discounts—without going back to the vice president I had reached directly. By the time I was done negotiating, my out-of-pocket cost was around $600. With a little bit of patience and following all the secret door techniques outlined in this book, I got almost exactly what I wanted.

$1,500 for an Hour's Worth of Messaging

Sixteen years ago, (that's right, 16 years ago), we purchased a high-end SUV. Since that time, we put over 143,000 miles on it. The warranty was only good for three years or 36,000 miles. Now, 16 years later the vehicle has gone from being valued at $80,000 to a value of $500. Even though we thoroughly enjoyed the vehicle, and my wife just won't let go of it, I felt this wasn't fair and that it ended up being a pretty bad investment. So, I went through my process to see what I could do about it.

Here's what happened. Through the secret door, I first found the vice president of customer service in Detroit as well as the names of several other vice presidents all on LinkedIn. I began by reaching out to each of them via InMail. My message was roughly as follows:

Dear (First name of Vice President),

I would like to express our tremendous disappointment owning our SUV over the years. In 2002 we bought a brand-new SUV with every available option. At first,

51

we loved the vehicle. However, right when the warranty ended, we started seeing everything go wrong with the vehicle: Air suspension, muffler, seat belts, leather seats all cracked and on and on. It was unbelievable. Today at 150,000 miles a large welded bolt fell off the frame and our mechanic said, "Don't even buy tires for this. It's only worth about $500!"

What?

Considering we have made payments over the years in excess of $80,000, I do believe this was the single worst investment we had ever made. Don't you agree? That said, we are now forced to buy another vehicle. My question to you is this: What, if anything, is your company prepared to do to keep me as a loyal customer after what we have been through?

Sincerely, Dan Portik

Owner/President **http://www.Bvsfilmproductions.com**

Avon, Ohio **440-653-9911**

Within a day, I received a response back from two of these vice presidents. One reached out by phone. The other sent the following email:

"Dan, thanks for reaching out! Please send me your detailed contact information and will have my team look into your concerns."

I sent back my contact information, and within one more day I received a call from someone at the next level down to get all the information about the vehicle. During this time, he asked for the vehicle's VIN number as well as a list of all the things that have gone wrong with it. I then sent the following message:

It was a pleasure speaking with you a few days ago and discussing our concerns with our SUV. Below you will find the following information you requested:

–   The last eight numbers of our VIN

–   A list of the key issues with the vehicle over the years, many of which occurred right after the warranty ran out

–   An amicable suggestion for resolution

Please review with your team and feel free to get back to me at your convenience.

VIN: xxxxxxxx

Key Issues/concerns:

–   Transmission blew at around 10,000 miles – Warranty work

–   Many of the front-end parts have been replaced already at around 50,000 – 60,000 miles

–   Brake lines replaced – 100,000 miles

–   Leather seats are cracked, ripped and shredded in all corners – Started around 60,000 miles and gets worse every year.

–   Air ride suspension blew out at around 60,000 miles

–   Battery replaced twice – Must be a short in the key area because you can't leave the keys in the car without it draining the battery. Started around 60,000 – 70,000 miles

–   Seat belt holder/harness on the back-passenger side fell apart and ripped a hole through the seat at 50,000 miles

- Radio has a loud crackling noise that gets louder as the engine RPM go faster. This started around 50,000 to 60,000 miles.

- Leaks oil from all engine gaskets – Noted two services ago

- Holes in muffler – Noted two services ago – (Normal wear and tear?)

- Passenger window motor broke – around 60,000 – 70,000 miles

- Rear defog rusted away and doesn't work – 60,000 – 70,000 miles

- Welded brackets that hold the body to the frame are falling off

- All fuel lines and many of the brackets holding lines up are rusting away – Last service - 143,000 miles

Our family mechanic said, after evaluating the underbody, not to even bother putting new tires on the vehicle because the SUV is only worth $500. That being said, this truck has been pampered with regular maintenance. My wife has driven it three miles a day to work and back for the entire time she has had the truck, and we have only taken two trips of around 2,000 miles each with it. We leased it brand new with every option available and truly loved it so much we purchased it at the end of the lease.

We estimated total payments with interest and repairs to be somewhere around $85,000 - $90,000. Now, I sincerely fear for the safety of my wife and our passengers. Her birthday is on January 27th. We would love to have this issue resolved by then. If we were able to acquire a much newer version of a loaded SUV that is more reliable with low-to-no miles and an extended warranty, (preferably black), we would be satisfied.

We are willing to pay $175/month with tax included and will trade in or donate our current SUV to the SUV Smithsonian. Considering our circumstances, we feel this is a fair resolution and will be keeping our family buying from your company for years to come.

Sincerely,

Dan Portik

Owner/President

After sending this email, I waited. I knew the next person to communicate in a negotiation typically concedes. I received a call back from one of the vice presidents. During the conversation, he said the company understands how we feel and is prepared to offer a special $1,500 coupon directly from corporate that would be over and beyond all other discounts offered by dealers.

Of course, I didn't expect to get a new vehicle out of this. Nor did I expect much of anything. After all, this is a 16-year-old vehicle that has suffered a fairly normal amount of wear and tear. My wife and I accepted the $1,500, which we thought was a fair offer. And it only took about an hour of my time to do the legwork and handle the correspondence.

In hindsight, I do wish I hadn't taken their first offer, but this was way more than we expected. This shows how important it is for companies to have loyal customers. Think of how many times you might have had an old car and wanted to call the manufacturer and tell them what you really felt about it. So, from now on, remember this story and go for it!

Getting What You Want...
and Keeping the Product

Some companies don't even want a defective product back. They just give you a full credit and pass that expense along to their vendors who make the product for them. I have been on the vendor side of this. If the company is big enough or places large enough orders, they will choose vendors who have a "no questions asked" return policy.

When my company was a vendor for a very large office supply chain, we received massive orders, massive checks and, of course, massive returns. In our case, we were selling CDs. So when a return came in to our client companies, it was cheaper for us to just tell them to throw it out on their end and credit the store chain, than go through the hassle of tracking and paying the postage to bring the product back to our location just to throw it away there.

This rings true with a custom embroidery and specialty items company online that I deal with all the time. They make custom shirts, mugs, jackets, and other promotional items. They will put your name and logo on just about anything. Whenever I have had a problem with any of the items I purchased from them, whether it was the color, size shape, or design, they gave me a full credit for it and told me to keep the items. Then they remade them at no charge to me or my company.

One time I ordered 15 hoodies for my employees worth several hundred dollars and they came in with the logo the wrong color. I called them up and the person on the other end said, "We will take care of this—no problem." I could hardly believe it. They sent 15 corrected jackets to me at no charge and said to keep the other 15. Wow! I was able to take them down to the local homeless shelter and made 15 people warm. I will never leave that company for as long as they are in business. I will NEVER leave that company as long as their service and products stay the same. And they know it.

Don't be surprised when you reach out to a company about a defective product and they do the same. For some, the hassle of dealing with returns is too great. They will gladly resolve your issue *and* prevent the hassle you would have of boxing and shipping the item back.

Nothing is Too Big

The most important thing I can tell you about these techniques is nothing is too big. You are only limited by your mind and your own beliefs. I am dead serious about that. If you truly believe you can achieve something with an online message, you will do it. YOU WILL.

But deep down, you know those feelings of doubt, fear, uncertainty? These feelings are very real. All I can say is to face them head on right now. Start with small steps and then slowly go bigger each time you try these methods. The key is to just get started right here and right now.

Sometimes you don't even know where your ideas will take you. Sometimes it opens up doors that you could only imagine!

One thing to remember is never to let emotions get the best of you when negotiating through online doors. In the case of the computer company, if I were to have sent a name-calling, arrogant email message to the sales representative I was dealing with, he would have most likely responded in kind and blown me off. My situation would have only gotten worse. You've heard the expression "you get more bees with honey than with vinegar", right? Well, there is good sense in that.

Before you write an email or online correspondence, take a breath, count to ten, and think about the person on the other end of your communication. Remember, in an email you cannot see emotion and you cannot feel feelings. Cold comments become colder when they're non-verbal. Mean comments can become lethal and even comments that you feel are acceptable can be taken the wrong way, and you would not even know.

In many cases, whoever you are communicating with is likely to have so many things going on at one time, especially if they are in customer service, that all they want to do is get your problem off their plate. What if you conversed with them as an understanding, patient friend with a problem you hope they can do you a favor and help you with? I can't tell you how many times I sent an email with a subject line of "favor to ask." Or "can you help me out?" And no matter what I asked (within reason) I got it without any questions asked.

There will be times when that is not the best approach. It's more likely when you're dealing with a lowly customer service representative that they'll offer you the least of what's available. If you're not happy with their solution, always ask to speak with a supervisor or manager. Your goal is not to belittle the first person you speak, with but to communicate with the right person who *can* give you what you want.

There is nothing worse than exhausting all your energy and techniques trying to negotiate with someone, only to find out that they are not able to help you with your issue. That being said, listen to the person on the other end of your communication. If it sounds like you're going around in circles or the individual just doesn't sound sure of themselves, or even worse, they are treating you poorly or disrespectfully, be polite and ask if you can speak to a supervisor.

Start with "Can you do me a favor and transfer me to your supervisor?" If the person says a supervisor won't be able to help, be polite and say something like: "I understand, but I would still like to speak to a supervisor about this." Sometimes they will make the transfer. Other times, they will say no one is available and ask for your number. They'll indicate that someone will get back to you, hoping you'll go away. About half the time, someone will return your call, but it will be when it's convenient for them. They'll have documentation of having made the call and that you weren't available. (This happens most often when the customer service call centers are across the country or on the other side of the world.) When asked to leave your number, be sure to indicate what time zone you're in and when you're available. Give them a wide time frame in which to reach you. Many customer service calls are recorded and having this aspect of your request documented could work to your advantage. Also include an email address in case the time zone difference truly is a challenge. Let them know you will watch for their message and respond in a timely manner. When you demonstrate a willingness to keep the lines of communication open, you're more likely to get a timely response.

Chapter 9

Expect Upgrades

One thing I have learned to expect in every transaction is upgrades. What this means is there are many opportunities at every turn to upgrade in any negotiation, whether online or in person. An upgrade is a little extra that the person on the other side of the table is willing to offer to do the deal, or let's say make your stay more comfortable at the local hotel. What are some of the factors that make this work? First and foremost is your ability to recognize these opportunities. They are everywhere if you really look for them.

Here is a quick example to give you an idea.

My wife and I attend a fundraiser every year around the same time. However, this year it fell on our 27th anniversary and was being held at a brand new, very nice hotel in our downtown area. I decided it would be nice to stay at the hotel that night after the fundraiser as a little gift to both of us. So, I booked the room and we went to the hotel.

Now in a normal situation, a couple would check in and take any room that the hotel would offer. But not for professional negotiators! They can see opportunity at every encounter.

We entered the lavish lobby of the hotel and were greeted by the concierge behind the desk. He was extremely friendly and customer service oriented. I knew at this point there was an opportunity. All the ingredients were there for a successful upgrade. So, as he was looking for rooms, I made a comment and asked a simple question. "Wow, this is a stunning hotel. I was wondering, it's our 27th anniversary. Is there anything you can do for us to make this a special night like a room upgrade?" Then I waited.

He replied first with "Well, let me see what I can do." This was followed by the sound of computer keys clicking away for a few seconds. He then said, "Are either of you afraid of heights?" We both looked at each other and smiled slightly and said "no." He said, "Okay, I just upgraded you to a top floor junior suite. Here are your keys. Just take the elevator to the very top." We thanked him greatly and said, "So far, the customer service here has been outstanding!" And when we got to our room it was beautiful, and the view was amazing. We were right on the city shoreline with a view for miles in every direction. All by using two simple statements.

Let's take a quick look at why this worked so well. First, you need to build the rapport with your customer service individual and become very friendly, so they want to help you. You want to be someone they will look forward to seeing the next time you come to the hotel.

In this situation, we had a customer service individual that was trained well and willing to do almost anything to make our stay perfect at their hotel. His desire to serve was easily recognizable and made things go smoothly.

Next, was the reason for him to justify the upgrade if he was ever asked about it. In this case, it was our anniversary. The situation could be the same if it were a birthday or any other special occasion. However, keep in mind it could have also been a not-so-special occasion. If you had poor service the last time you were in the hotel or even in the competition's hotel, a good customer service person will want to make things better this time. That conversation could have gone like this: "You know we stayed at the hotel down the street last week and I have got to tell you, the service there was terrible. Is there anything special you can do for us to make us life-long clients of *your* hotel chain?"

The next part was the timing of the request. I waited until he was searching for a room after we built rapport with him and knew he liked us. Then the request: I started first with a sincere complement about the property and then asked a specific question with a suggestion as to what would make our stay special. I requested a "room upgrade." But that could have easily been switched to a complimentary breakfast, dinner or really anything within reason that the hotel could offer.

The last part of this request was the silence. That is the period after you make your request where you don't say a word. (This is the hardest part.) There is a saying in sales. After you say your close, the next person who speaks owns whatever you are selling. This is true in negotiations as well.

After you ask for something in a negotiation, the next person who speaks, usually, is the one who concedes or compromises their position. In other words, if I would have said something after my request while he was typing like, "It would really mean a lot to us," or "Wow, we never stayed in a hotel as nice as this one" or "Please, please see what you can do," that would have diluted the sincerity of my request and our position as valued guests they would like to have return. If I did that, in his mind as he was typing looking for a room, he might be thinking things like. "This guest is trying too hard to please me and is talking a lot. What if he starts bragging about a great deal he got from me and it gets back to my boss? Or what if he goes to the bar in the hotel and drinks too much and starts a scuffle. I can't afford to have that happen on my shift." The next words out of his mouth might have been, "So sorry, it looks like we are completely full." Have you ever heard that before?

I would say, at least in my experience, if all the ingredients are there, this works about 75% of the time. I have done this for simple things like getting an extra scoop of ice cream. I've used the strategy all the way up to a week in a penthouse suite in some of the nicest hotels in the world. You just need to ask, and make sure you're speaking with someone who can give you what you want.

I know this was an "in person" negotiation. However, the strategy has and does work just as well online.

Ask for Demo or Floor Models

Have you ever asked for a floor model or demo unit of something? It never hurts to ask for the demo model or floor model. Let's say you are in a department store and you see that there is a great recliner on the floor that you have sat in that is just right. You tell the sales representative you would like to purchase that one. The representative might say, "Sorry that's the last unit that we have and it's a floor model." This can now be opportunity knocking. All that is left is a floor model. If he says they can't get any more, that means they have no reason to keep the floor model on the floor, right?

You would then ask to speak to the manager and tell them you would like to purchase that one. Nine times out of ten they will say yes. Often, they will give a discount to take that one off the floor. At that point you can set the terms of your negotiation, because they want to get rid of it. The good news is it's sold as new and in addition to getting the discount, you will get a full warranty for the unit. You will never know unless you ask. Right?

Chapter 10

Using the Secret Door for Employment

Even when looking for employment, the secret door techniques and online rules apply. In most cases, if done correctly, you can reach anyone you want, bypass the mountains of resumes, and go right to the decision maker. It may not get you hired, but it will get you noticed. And really that's half the battle when job hunting. How can an employer know what a great person you are if your resume is buried under a stack of online resumes? I have used these same strategies on several occasions to get jobs.

Here are the basic steps to doing so.

1. Your online profile must match the job you're seeking. Many employers look to LinkedIn to check your business profile, and places like Facebook and Twitter to see what your social behavior is. That's right. The key word is behavior! If you want to have a chance for a job, behave online (and off for that matter).

    As for your LinkedIn profile, make sure that you have all your ducks in a row. Your profile picture, profile description, and all the areas must be completely filled out. Everything should be grammatically correct. Include a professional video of yourself and maybe some video testimonials from previous employers, friends, or business associates. There is no better way for an employer to meet you before they meet you than by a video.

2. Facebook and Twitter – These social media platforms must be squeaky clean. Post no foul language, no suggestive pictures, no bashing. Stick with happy, friendly photos of

you and your friends in positive social environments. I know, to some this could be a shock and a lot of work to clean up. However, if you are serious about getting a job, you need to face facts and reality. The fact is most employers want to hire people that are happy and approachable. If they don't see that in your online profile, you can bet they aren't going to call you for an interview. And if that goes against what you believe in, maybe you have some soul searching to do.

So now that you have your personal and business profile looking great, let's go fishing. First, know what you want from a prospective employer. Are you looking for an in-person interview, or an opportunity to work remotely where the interview would be conducted over the phone? Next, think about where you want to work. Does it matter whether your employer is local or across the country? What is the position you are looking for?

If you are looking to wash cars, you might want to pick the top 20 car wash companies in your area and send a LinkedIn InMail to the owners of the car wash saying how great a worker you would be, punctual, clean cut, and honest. And tell them after they review your information, you could start as early as tomorrow.

If you are looking for, say, a vice president of marketing position in New York city, follow the same format, only reach out to that specific demographic with an InMail or online correspondence that relates to that company.

Here is an example of what I did personally to get hired sight unseen with an advertising agency 1,500 miles away, without even speaking with them.

While I was between positions of running my own advertising agency for 20 years and starting my current video production/content marketing company, my wife thought it might be good for me to take a job working for another company. I was trying to figure out the next steps in re-inventing myself (as many 50-somethings say).

I first made sure my profile was spotless and had plenty of videos and customer testimonials from my previous business in it. I made sure everything online looked perfect. I then started fishing.

I reached out to the owner of the top 50 advertising agencies online and made an introduction as a candidate for sales and marketing. I didn't go to job search sites and fill out applications that I know would get lost in a sea of other electronic resumes. While those services have helped many to learn about open positions, I didn't like the idea that I would never have a clue who might be looking at my resume, what mood they were in, or what criteria was required to even be considered for a position.

Think about that for a minute. When you put your resume on an online job placement board, look at all the variables that come into play that are working against you. As a business owner myself in the past, I knew when I put my own help-wanted ad on an online job board, it became a daunting task to review all the resumes I received. And I'll be honest with you, after about the first 100 resumes, let's just say my filtering process became rather stringent, and there was a good chance I passed up several qualified prospects just because I was tired of looking or had other things on my mind. I knew if that was happening with me, it would be happening with the person on the other end as well.

With this in mind, I decided to stack the odds in my favor. First, I needed to find out who could get me what I wanted (a job in sales for an advertising agency.) Then I had to have a message that was appealing enough to make a case to hire me.

My process went as follows. I knew I had great success reaching out to professionals on LinkedIn, and I knew that the buck usually stops at the owner of a business. So I went to LinkedIn and reached out to owners of medium-sized advertising agencies on my side of the country.

Using a simple message, I introduced myself, told what I had to offer and how I felt I could be of value to them. Then I did the numbers. Out of 50 messages, I received 10 responses. From the ten, I talked with two of them over the phone and was hired by one out-of-state ad agency (sight unseen) to head up a Cleveland division of their agency. I worked with them for about one year as a managing director of the division.

Altogether the process may have involved five emails, four phone calls and approximately two hours of my time. Now if I were to have just thrown my hat in the ring in an online job placement board, what would have been the odds of this company finding me? Well, I know exactly what the odds would have been—zero! Want to know how I know this? Because this company wasn't even looking for someone! That's right, my message sparked the owner to think about the potential of opening up a division in the Cleveland area. Between my messaging and phone conversations, I was able to convince him to do just that.

At no point did I send anyone a resume. I simply had my LinkedIn profile looking perfect with more information than a typical resume. I didn't try to reach out to the employment department or HR department that has a sea of qualified (and unqualified) resumes bombarding their company email account. I didn't use a specific form or set of guidelines to even be considered as a candidate for a position. I simply went to the owner—the one who is in charge, who doesn't have to answer to anybody but maybe shareholders. I had nothing to lose and everything to gain by doing so.

Chapter 11

How I Became a Best-Selling Author through the Secret Door

Please note that in the beginning of this quest, I knew nothing about the publishing business or how to write a book. Once again, I'll say that nothing's impossible. The only thing that holds any of us back is our own fear of trying...and knowledge of effective strategies like those in this book.

The creation of this opportunity is what finally convinced me how well my strategies and techniques worked for getting the attention of others and getting what I wanted from them.

I know that the term "best-selling author" is a term that is used loosely these days. There are ways of manipulating the algorithms and odds of getting on a best-seller list. However, my first book became an Amazon #1 Best Selling book in several categories in two countries and 2# in the USA in several categories within two months of its launch. These are facts and we have the screen shot from Amazon to prove it.

Believing I had a solid concept for a book and proof that my strategies were working, I reached out to my sales mentor and hero in sales, internationally-known speaker, sales trainer and best-selling author, Tom Hopkins. I grew up learning and benefitting from his sales programs and learned everything I know about closing from him.

I found Tom Hopkins on LinkedIn and decided to send an InMail to him explaining my new sales concept of closing sales without ever speaking with my clients. All kinds of things went through my head before I hit the send button. "How dare I think I am good enough to reach out to one of the greatest sales trainers and show him something about sales" or " I never wrote or published anything, who do I think I am?" or "What if he mocks me or laughs at me for thinking I could even consider speaking with him?" and on and on.

Sounds pretty silly, right?

Well, not when you're about to do it. Your mind conjures up all kinds of crazy thoughts. In the end I decided and said to myself, "what do I really have to lose?" And the answer that kept coming back was "NOTHING!" So, I hit send, and a great wave of terror and relief came over me. Deep down, I felt it was a great idea, but had very little faith anything would come of it. Then to my surprise, the very next day he responded and said to reach out to his vice president of business development. He suggested they would evaluate the idea and see if it made sense, as he was seeking opportunities to co-author with others! What?!

I sent her a similar email and within a week or so she said she reviewed the concept with Tom and asked if we could develop a deeper outline of what I was thinking. I couldn't believe it. Not knowing anything about writing a book, I did just that to the best of my ability. It wasn't anything formal, just a draft of the topics and how I had used some of Tom's sales strategies within the structure of my process.

Once the concept was clear, they reached out to one of their publishers, who thought the concept had merit. The next thing you know, I was signed with an international publisher and was on my way to co-authoring a book with my life-long sale mentor, Tom Hopkins! Tom and his team helped every step of the way in writing the book and 17 months later, we launched our co-authored book titled, "Fill Your Funnel" internationally.

Even after developing and launching the book, sales were a bit sparse at first. We only sold about 30 units in the first month. Then I remember what the owner of our publishing company said to us. "Writing a successful book nowadays is 5% creativity and 95% marketing." With that, he discussed several options to market the book. But one he said by far was the fastest way to authors' success. This was an organization called Book Bub. They are a group that reviews and hand-picks (mostly best seller) books and offers them at a feature price to their vast readership of millions. This intrigued me. The publisher also said it is almost impossible for a new author to get featured. There was that word, "impossible," again. So, what did I do? I used the strategies in the book to reach out to the people at Book Bub.

I went through the check boxes. First, how do I look online, am I reputable, do I look believable? Box checked! Next, find people that can give you what you want and ask them for it. In this situation, Book Bub used a form you filled out to submit your book. However, before I did that, I knew there was more that had to be done, or I was just going to get lost in the sea of other books that were being reviewed. With limited credentials, the odds of success were slim to none that this book would get their attention.

I went on LinkedIn and found all of the owners and founders of Book Bub and sent each of them a LinkedIn InMail message. In it, I explained how I wanted to promote and coordinate a marketing campaign to drive traffic to their site when the book was approved, and how I would like to show a video trailer of the book. I gave them a link to the video trailer I developed. Then I filled out the application and sent it in. A few weeks went by and I thought nothing of it. And then, out of the blue, I got an email stating my book was approved for the feature campaign! Really? Wow. Yes, now I knew without a doubt, this concept worked every time! Three weeks later the book was offered to 500,000 business readers, sold several thousand copies overnight and achieved Amazon #1 best seller status in two countries in several categories and 2# in the United States. I became a best-selling author!

So, the next time you have an idea for a book or concept, ask yourself. "Who should I reach out to?" And, "What have I got to lose?"

Chapter 12

The Devil is in the Details

To gain the most benefit from the secret online door and negotiating, the devil is in the details. I already mentioned how important it is to be organized. The importance of the details comes into play when doing your research as well.

You may determine that there are several doors that lead to the opportunity you want to create or the result you desire. You can use many doors at the same time. You just may need to be strategic about how and when to use them. Be prepared to do the numbers. With a big company, don't just contact one owner, founder, vice president, or higher-up. Contact as many people as you can that might help your situation. It's about the numbers and getting the right person to help you get what you want.

You want to reach the type of person that has the right combination of clout and customer service to make things happen. And in many cases, it takes more than one contact to accomplish this. The higher up in a company you are, the more things that are put on your shoulders to get completed in a shorter timeframe. It only makes sense to use as many doors as you can.

One user of the strategies in this book reached out to four different executives in a large corporation. She let each know the names of the others she had contacted. This caused those four executives to have a conversation about the opportunity that may never have occurred if she had reached out to one person or contacted them one at a time. Those executives then reached out to her to arrange a call to discuss the opportunity. Who do you think had the upper hand in that negotiation?

Keep in mind, executives are busy, they are doing back-to-back meetings, flying to different stores or locations, working on reports, and so on. With this in mind, many of them might either ignore your plea for help or pass it on to someone else. That's why you do the numbers and keep track of the details of every contact. Out of 10 or 20 vice presidents, you might find two that might respond to you personally. And when they do, you now have a very direct and powerful way to getting exactly what you want out of a negotiation. Be prepared to research and use several secret doors.

Using Other Forms of Communication

In some cases, when you are dealing with higher authorities in a company, you might find that they like to communicate in a different way. You may initially connect with them via LinkedIn or their company email, but for expediency sake, the communication needs to switch to text messaging. Texting can be great because it gives you an inside track that very few people can reach. I have seen this with cable company repairmen all the way up to vice presidents of marketing for very large computer corporations.

When you can text right to their mobile device, you know they will get your message in a timely manner, and in many cases they will get back to you right away. However, remember not to abuse this privilege. There is nothing worse than being texted a complaint. Remember, texting is a personal place. It's where kids text to get a ride home from soccer practice or where spouses keep each other informed of personal matters throughout the day. Once you are allowed into that space, only use it when absolutely necessary or when asked to do so. Always ask if it is okay to continue to communicate that way.

This goes for any other form of communication. If your higher authority is a phone person and requests you call them via the phone, call them. Whatever way makes it easier for them, do it.

You might say, "Wait a minute, I thought I was in charge here and they are supposed to listen to me and help me." Well, you are half right. If you do this right, you will be in charge and they will want to listen to you. By being polite and respecting their preferred mode of communication, you are building a level of trust with them. The higher up the food chain you go in a company, the more an executive expects to be treated professionally. If you don't, they will most likely pawn you off to someone at your level of communication skill or lack thereof. Be nice and be respectful and you will see great success in most cases.

The Difference between a Professional Negotiator and a Poor One

You've seen or heard them. The poor communicators and negotiators. They are the people that blurt out their demands, cut you off in the middle of a sentence, or don't have any respect for your time. When you are dealing on an executive level or really any level online, one of the main things that will set you apart from the poor negotiators will be the fact that you will be highly respectful of others.

When you are conversing with an executive, ask them if this a good time to speak or if there's a better time. You might find once you reach the right person, that the nicer and more respectful you are of their time, the more they will do for you. This has been true time and time again for me. They will respect you for being a professional and keeping the conversation that way. Keep your emotions in check and go with "just the facts" of the situation.

Learn to Spot a Poser

It happens in some companies when you ask to speak with a supervisor that your call is transferred to another person at the same level who poses as a supervisor. This tactic, while unprofessional, is used to fend off unhappy customers. The person may acknowledge your unhappiness with what the customer service representative has told you but will stick to the "company policy" line.

I have been told the following: "There is no one in the company that you can go higher to and they are the final decision maker in the company." Really? The person in customer service is the only person in the company that can make a decision on my issue? Until you win this person over or get past him to the next level, that person holds your fate in his hands. He or she can either help you, or hang up on you and add more time and effort to your side of the equation. Remember the poser supervisor feels they are in charge and can make decisions even though they can't. Another reason they stall you is to cover their tracks, or because they are afraid if they do give you to a real supervisor, they will be found out as being a less than attentive employee and they will get in trouble.

How do you deal with a poser? You treat them like the king or queens they feel they are. Maybe start the conversation by saying: "I am so sorry the inconvenience this is causing you. However, if there is any way you might be able to take a few minutes to look at this or if you might be able to have one of your assistants take care of this little issue, it would be a great favor to me and I would be forever grateful." Yep, groveling works with some people.

Or you might say: "Would there be any way you could bring this issue up at your next executive managers meeting?" I know, I know. This person is most likely being rude to you, condescending and pompous. And if you are like me, you want to reach right through the internet and punch their lights out! Well don't.

If they say, "No, I am sorry, I just don't have time to help you out," maybe you've truly reached the wrong person and you change tactics. Rather than asking for help in resolving your issue, ask for help in connecting with the right person.

Never Burn Bridges

When working with anyone online, don't burn bridges. Why? Because you never know when you will need those people down the road. They say on an average, everybody knows around 250 people. These include family, friends, relatives and business associates. So, when dealing with someone, especially if they are in a position to help you and you are using your business name, always stay professional. All you really have in the business world is your reputation, and when you get known as a bully or somebody with less than a perfect demeanor, it's very hard to change that. Also, you never know who that person on the other end of your communication might know that you need to know. If you're a jerk to them, you'll never get an introduction to someone else they know.

Be Appreciative

This simple strategy goes a long way. When someone helps you, give them praise and recognition for doing so. If someone goes the extra mile to ensure you are happy or that your issue is resolved, thank them and let their supervisor or boss know what a great job they did. Answer customer survey questions. Send thank you notes. That bit of positivity might be the only bright spot in that person's day, week, or month! Praise can go a long way in this world, considering there is so little of it out there.

Be Fair

This should be able to go unsaid, but I want to bring it up. Never take more than you agree to in a negotiation. If someone makes a mistake on calculations or pricing or anything that may give you more than agreed upon, correct them and take only your fair share.

If you ever have the opportunity to correct a vendor or rep because they gave you more than you agreed upon by mistake, consider yourself blessed. This is a big opportunity to show your true colors and show someone else on this planet that you can be completely and unconditionally trusted. When you do the right thing and correct them and take only your fair share, there will never be a question of your honesty unless you give them a reason not to trust down the road. In my experience, I have always found if I do the right thing in one area, I have always, always received more than my share in other areas in my life.

It Doesn't Hurt to Be Bold

Being bold by far can be one of the hardest yet most rewarding things to do in a negotiation. Having a nothing-to-lose-and-everything-to-gain attitude will allow you to create a higher level of success in everything you do.

When I was a child, my father used to find amazing deals on used cars, restore them, and sell them for sometimes as much as ten times what he paid for them. Some would call his techniques unorthodox, and others might consider them to be on the verge of being intrusive. I called it bold and now use his techniques every day.

For example, he and my mother would drive around different neighborhoods and when he saw a car parked on a lawn or along the side of a house with grass around the wheels, he would go up to the door of the house, knock, and ask the person who answered if they were interested in selling it. He was prepared to offer them cash on the spot. He would typically offer about one-third what the car was worth. Sometimes he was told to get off the property as my mother would sink deep into the passenger seat in embarrassment. But other times, he was not. In some cases, the husband would say "No way. That car is a classic and is worth way more than that." However, when my Dad pulled out the money, the wife would say, "Get rid of that eye sore now. We have braces to pay for this month!"

In some cases, they had grass under the wheels because the current owner was unable to start it. These folks would often reply, "If you can start it, you can take it." With that, my father as a mechanic would bring out a small vial of gas and poor it directly in the carburetor, and with a turn of the key a few times, it would often start right up. White clouds of smoke would billow out of the exhaust where water and condensation had collected in the pipes. Then, after about 10 minutes, he would drive the car home, with my mother following in our car!

My dad, in his own world, was a bold visionary. He would then begin the process of restoring the car that he would eventually park in our front yard with a "for sale" sign on it. Wow, professional negotiator, restoration specialist, and last but definitely not least, closer. I didn't know it at the time, but I learned a lot from him and use his techniques successfully every day in my businesses.

The question now is: where can you be bold in your life? Look at all the places the secret online doors might take you.

You now have the strategies you need to increase the odds of winning when you are brave enough to be bold. You have the map to the secret door to anywhere you want to go online, and the knowledge to forge a key to open it and reach anyone and get anything you desire from them. Expect the impossible and believe you can do it.

I'm here to tell you there is nothing stopping you. Nothing. It may take some practice and patience, but it is worth it in the end. Negotiating is a series of small victories that lead to a win-win for everybody. And online negotiation is done the same way. No one should leave a negotiation feeling they got shorted or ripped off. Use the secret door to your advantage. However, don't abuse its power.

With this unique power comes unique responsibility. If you are trying to use it just to meet a celebrity for bragging rights, or "ask for a million dollars" for no reason or purpose, you will get shut down before you get started. The door, if you even find it, will stay locked. You will pound and pound and no one will answer. However, if you use the door with humble honesty with the purpose to help people, or right what you know in your heart is wrong, the door will open wide and those you request assistance from will happily help you. Think about all the great things that can happen when you say, "What have I got to lose?" and use the strategies to open doors to opportunities you previously thought closed to you. Be willing to look around for grass under tires, and be bold enough to do what no one else will do. You won't regret it.

Good luck on your journey to find the secret door to *your* success. It's out there waiting for you!